D0401905

Renewable Referrals

How to Cultivate More Profits

Debbie DeChambeau, Ray L. Perry,
Jeff Stec, Rosie Taylor,
Kelly Weppler Hernandez,
Dawn Westerberg

Renewable Referrals

Table of Contents

Foreword

A Case for Collaborative Coopetition

During the past five years or so I've been in the unique position of watching the six authors of this book join my Duct Tape Marketing Consultant network. Each joined at a different time and eventually formed what I believe is a brilliant demonstration of what it means to have strategic partners. This group originally came together as part of a peer-to-peer workshop. Who would think this group of marketing consultants would continue to meet weekly for over a year since then? They regularly collaborate on projects, share knowledge and become a source of referrals for each other. Despite the fact that each of them is a marketing consultant, they do not see themselves as competing and their spirit of community is evident by the consistent results they achieve as a group. I'm proud to see members of my Consultant network working together so closely and reaping the biggest benefit of what it means to be part of the Duct Tape Marketing network: our community.

After reading Renewable Referrals, I'm pleased to see how they took the concept of strategic partnering for referrals and dove in providing the reader with a plan, practical advice and examples. This group, in its own weekly practice, has become its own internal referral network--demonstrating the power of 'word of mouth' as they continue to refer and collaborate successfully. Most people would hesitate or avoid working in a group within their own industry and yet these six marketing consultants: Dawn, Debbie, Jeff, Kelly, Ray and Rosie embrace it. They would even tell you that it is actually a strength to have members at different levels of experience and skill sets. One person will learn a new tool or tactic and share it with the rest. Sometimes this shortens the learning curve or causes one of them to pivot to something completely different. It's evident that they support each other in all aspects to continuously become better consultants and business owners.

At last year's Annual Duct Tape Marketing Consultant Gathering, two of the authors committed to write a book as an action step in 2014. Little did they know at the time that it would end up being a shared vision for the members of their weekly group. As the author of multiple books, I can tell you that writing is no small venture, so I am happy to see these consultants pool their resources to work on this project together and get it completed.

What I enjoyed most about this book is the practical approach it takes towards strategic partnering for referrals. While my own book "The Referral Engine" gave readers a full framework for referral marketing, this book focuses on one of the most consistent sources of work, which is partnering. In the spirit of the Duct Tape brand, this book is about the practical nuts and bolts of creating that plan and provides a road map for creating those strategic relationships. Renewable Referrals takes a systematic approach to referrals and breaks it down into actionable pieces that will repeatedly produce consistent results year after year.

I am excited to see this tangible result of what these six individual consultants created collectively. Alone they have different talents and strengths, yet together they stand shoulder to shoulder to share some authentic advice about how to go about growing your business. Renewable Referrals provides those simple steps to creating the most powerful referral network possible. My hope is that you take what you learn from these pages and start acting on a plan to begin as soon as you read the last words.

John Jantsch
Author, Duct Tape Marketing and The Referral Engine

Introduction

"If I could just get more 'at bats' I could close more business. The problem is I don't have as many opportunities to get in front of prospective customers as I'd like."

You?

We hear it all the time.

In fact, "more opportunities to be in front of prospects" is probably the single most common item on business owners' wish lists when we sit down with them to develop a marketing plan.

Of course, that big wish is dwarfed by a much bigger one – more revenue. But increased revenue flows from access to more opportunities, so that's where we focus.

Cold and Warm
There are only two kinds of new customers you'll ever find: cold and warm.

Cold leads have never heard of you or your business. They may not even know they need or want what you sell, yet. To reach them, you'll need an effective demand generation or lead generation plan.

It will take time to nurture these cold leads and gradually get them motivated to buy from you… and the more expensive your products and services are, the longer that process is going to take. After all, no one makes an impulse buy of products and services priced five figures and above – especially from someone they don't know, like (yet), or trust.

The warm ones are another story. They already trust you, at least a little bit.

The warm leads come to you as referrals. Someone who already knows, likes, and trusts you sent them your way. By the time they've entered your orbit, they're already prequalified and motivated to buy from you. They've heard you can solve their problem with your products or services. Whoever sent them your way has just fast-forwarded the sales cycle for you.

Referrals are the best leads to work because they are pre-qualified. They usually zip through a much shorter sales cycle. Sometimes, they're already so sold on doing business with you that they don't even look at your competitors. All in all, they've got a lower cost of sales, and are by far the best way to bring revenue into your business quickly.

I Used to Do That!

When we go through this explanation of cold and warm leads, and how those warm leads show up, a light bulb goes off and business owners remember back to when they started their businesses. They got their businesses up and running on the strength of referrals.

It worked great!

Until the flow of referrals stopped, anyway – and the only reason the referrals stopped coming in was that there was no system for getting more.

That's what this book is all about.

Wait – you just flinched… and we know why.

You might be getting nervous right now. You've probably heard how important it is to ask for referrals from your happy customers. You may have gotten the standard advice on getting more referrals by doing the following:

- Establish a standard operating process where every transaction is followed by the request for referrals.
- Starting every new engagement with "the talk" in which you lay out the expectation that when you've done a great job for your client, you'll expect they'll cough up a few names of people you can contact to sell to.
- Checking in by email on a regular basis to see if your existing clients have anyone to send your way.
- Publically acknowledging people and companies who send referrals to you in the presence of others who might take the hint and follow suit.
- Even asking for referrals from your own prospects who ultimately say no to your products or services.

There are lots of people who do all that and get great results. But it's not an approach everyone feels comfortable taking. In fact, maybe you'd rather gnaw your own arm off than reach out like that to get referrals – and for sure, you'd rather forfeit the highly desirable leads that could be yours through referral marketing than to be so direct about asking.

We've got you covered.

See, when you develop a referral system, it's like owning a qualified-lead-generating machine. It's such an important tactic that we knew there had to be a way to do it that didn't feel awkward.

Plus, your clients will be sure to refer you if they feel comfortable doing so. And even your most-connected clients will only have so many prospective referrals, anyway.

A referral system built only on client recommendations can work, if you can get comfortable with it; but a referral system built the way you're about to discover not only feels a lot less awkward, it's also got the potential to send you an endless stream of new business. It's renewable!

We call it 'renewable' referrals because in developing referral partners (who know exactly what kind of prospects to send your way) you are developing 'gifts that keep on giving' – business relationships that continually, automatically renew your pipeline with opportunities that are highly likely to close.

That's how you get more 'at bats'.

Before we get going much further, you'd probably like to get a high-level overview of who we are, and why we're sharing this information with you.

The six of us authors, the Marketing Results Crew, are Duct Tape Marketing Consultants. Over a year ago, we decided to start meeting together weekly by phone, and once a year in person in a mastermind group. We discuss marketing strategies, technologies, tools, and best practices as we grow our own businesses and work with our clients. We enjoy meeting regularly, bringing challenges, ideas, questions, and innovations to the group to share, get feedback, and gain perspective. We come from all across the nation, and have a wide range of backgrounds and specialties in marketing.

We noticed that our clients faced some common challenges – usually around the need to generate more qualified leads. While many of our clients had successfully used referral marketing early on, very few remembered to use that tactic as their businesses matured. Most were still getting referrals now and then, but none had really systematized the process to the point they had a referral marketing program in place.

Building and launching a referral marketing program is one of the most sensible and productive marketing initiatives any business can undertake. It takes time to create and see results, but it's a tactic that's never too late to start using.

No matter how long ago your last ideal customer was referred to you, this book will help you learn how to get that to happen more often.

So, Why Referrals?

"No thanks, my sales funnel is full."

No one. Ever.

Six out of six authors of this book agree:

The number one reason business owners seek out marketing help is a dangerously low – or completely empty – sales pipeline funnel.

We suspect we're not alone.

We never get calls saying, "Oh, things are going great! We have all the business we can handle. We just want to make it better."

Nope.

999 times out of 1,000, a call from a business owner is a cry for help.

We aren't doctors. We don't play them on TV. We didn't even stay at a Holiday Inn Express last night. But when an SOS call comes in from a business owner, no matter which of us gets the call, the next step is an examination.

"Thinking about the business you have closed, what was your best source of leads?" we'll ask. We wait patiently while you think through your business history, customer-by-customer. And then, like clockwork, we hear the same answer:

The lead was referred by someone.

Referrals: It's how businesses are born.

Think back to the early days of your business. Where did your first customers come from?

Referrals.

That's almost always the answer. In fact, most businesses launch on the strength of referrals.

And it makes sense, really.

Think about it. Why did you start your business?

Maybe you saw a gaping hole in the market. There was some product or service that you knew you could deliver better than what everyone else was doing.

Or, maybe after years working in corporate, you got frustrated with the slow-moving nature of large companies. You wanted to zig, zag, and zoom, innovating and running lean and mean, and knew that was impossible in the corporate setting. You yearned to escape the constraints of the corporate quagmire, the red tape, the analysis paralysis, and enjoy the agility of exceling on your own.

You just knew you were in a better position to truly serve the needs and desires of your ideal customers.

So you wouldn't shut up about your business. Really. Anyone who'd stand still long enough – didn't matter if you knew them or not, if they were within arm's reach you at least thought about telling them about your business. You were worse than a new puppy owner whipping out pictures at the slightest sign of interest.

It's okay. It's what excitement does, and enthusiasm is the fuel of entrepreneurism.

Plus, it worked.

You shared your vision, which included who you wanted to serve and how. People took notice and started sending potential customers your way. You worked those leads and built a base of customers.

Pairing Perfectly-Suited Partners

I have worked with several business owners in the legal services space. Attorneys are particularly great referral partners for other attorneys. Because this is a group of professionals that truly understands the need to hire professionals with specialized skills, they can appreciate the expertise of others with distinct knowledge. In this situation, the family law attorney is a great source of referrals for the estate planning attorney and vice versa.

Inviting a business law attorney makes a great addition to this referral network because ensuring the paperwork around a business is sound is also of great importance to those who are proactive in estate planning. Together, the various legal specialties can be an excellent source of referral business.

Kelly Weppler Hernandez
WH & Associates, Marketing Strategists

Fish in a barrel, anyone?

When a prospect comes to you through a referral, they are automatically more qualified than someone you approach or someone who comes to you through any form of advertising.

There's probably nobody better equipped to explain why that is than a Duct Tape Marketer, which means, boy, are you in luck. All six of us behind this book are Duct Tape Marketing Consultants. This is a topic we deal with daily, and with our combined experience of more than a century in marketing, we can tell you referral marketing really works.

Why is a referred lead a more qualified lead? It's got to do with the progression of your relationship with them. That relationship moves from a starting point where your prospect has never heard about you and would never even consider doing business with you all the way to the point where they become your customer.

Along that path, your relationship passes certain milestones – and with each one, the point of sale moves closer. These steps are Know-Like-Trust-Try-Buy-Repeat-Refer. This is a concept John Jantsch of Duct Tape Marketing created, called the Marketing Hourglass™.

The early stages of your sales funnel are lead generation and qualification. Those two take your prospect through the Know-Like-Trust-Try phases of the sequence.

Implementing these necessary steps keeps your prospect headed in the right direction. Unfortunately, even though it's all moving in the general direction of a purchase, this progression can take a very long time. Waiting for them to pop out of the other end of your sales funnel is going to be a major test of your patience – and it's likely to take longer than you can really afford, especially if your sales funnel is anemic or empty.

Not to bring up bad memories, but think back to the last time you met what seemed like a hot prospect at a trade show, or the last time you attended a networking event and collected a stack of business cards so thick you could have single-handedly run a ticker tape parade. You had every intention of growing your network, making the time you spent at the event worthwhile.

Smart business owner that you are, you followed up with these leads… IF you could get through to them.

What did you learn when you finally reached them? Something that sounded like this: "Oh. Yeah. So, I was just gathering information. I'll let you know if and when I'm ready to pull the trigger."

They're not ready. They're not in BUY mode.

They may be, someday, if you nurture them and gradually nudge them further into the sales funnel. That way, when they are ready, they'll think of you. But it's not going to happen today, tomorrow, or even next week. It could be months or years before they're ready.

Of course, it's a different story entirely if there's a referral involved.

A lead that comes in as a referral is probably the customer of someone you know (we'll call this your referral partner). In the course of working with the customer, your referral partner learns that the customer is struggling with something that's holding their business back. Your referral partner knows you'd be able help this customer overcome the challenge, tells their customer about you and your products or services, and why it's likely you could be a huge help in meeting this challenge.

Your referral partner has just qualified a lead for you.

Whoosh, that lead just zipped through the Know-Like-Trust progression. It's their positive first-hand experience with your referral partner, all-powerful trusted third-party endorsement that makes all the difference.

Because they trust your referral partner, they now also trust you.

Think about it. This is a pretty sweet deal, because basically you've done absolutely NOTHING to earn their trust or preference. If your referral partner hadn't intervened, you'd probably never have even crossed paths with this potential customer.

Even if you'd been lucky enough to identify them (and that's a long shot), educating them on your products and services on your own through direct marketing might take months and hundreds of dollars spent on marketing and follow up, with no guarantee of closing the deal.

Referral leads are ideal because they are:

- Prequalified by someone who knows you and what you do.
- Predisposed to trust you because they trust someone who trusts you.

- Perfectly timed because they come to you at the exact moment they've got a problem they need you to solve.

That puts you in a perfect position. You've got a direct add for your pipeline.

Referral sales move faster.

Thanks to your referral partner, your qualified referral lead has been escorted from the comparatively murky, foggy land of Know-Like-Trust to the far sunnier land of Try-Buy.

Do you see the enormous amount of time and money your referral partner just saved you?

You get to zip right past all the tedium of sifting through dozens of unqualified leads in the hope of finding a qualified lead, and skip right to the good part – where you've got a new customer.

Most business owners know the feeling of getting on an endless round of phone calls, answering questions and objections about your products and services, spending hours developing proposal documents, then revising those proposal documents, rounding up and publishing testimonials, preparing a list of references, running through product demonstrations, negotiating prices….

And losing out to a competitor, or more frequently, stalemating with your prospect making no decision other than to not move forward at this time.

There's no guarantee you'll be spared all that when you get leads referred to you, but experience has shown that you're much more likely to close these opportunities, faster.

Nobody minds doing all that if the odds are higher than average that you'll win that prospect's business.

That's the worst case scenario… but watch this.

Sometimes your pre-sale investment (your time and money) is radically reduced. Especially if this prospect has been struggling with the problem for a while, they've probably checked out various solutions – and haven't ever found someone they Know-Like-Trust enough to move the process forward. Chances are, at some point in the past, they've talked to your competitors and done all their data gathering on their dime. When nothing seemed like the right solution at the right time, they fell back into the position of 'no decision.'

They did nothing, and their problem didn't go away. In fact, it's probably gotten worse.

You enter the scene in the role of the expert, the problem solver, the magic wand – described that way by someone this prospect already trusts. Instantly, their fear, uncertainty, and doubt pretty much disappears and they're willing to move forward quickly with you with much more peace of mind.

**Referrals put you in a better competitive position
(if there are any other competitors).**

Too often, if you are competing for business with multiple competitors, all things being equal, it could come down to who's willing to drop their price to win the sale. So now, on top of the cost of marketing and the time you've invested in the sales cycle you are in a position to lose more margin in order to win the business.

When business is referred to you, you are in a better competitive position and there may not be any competition at all. With that magical transference of trust that happens with referrals, all you've got to do now is prove you can solve the problem – and that's always better than the race to the bottom that ensues when price-slashing becomes the name of the game.

With referrals, you'll lower your cost of sales.

When you receive a referral, most of the time this prospect was not even on your radar. You've invested exactly ZERO money to buy a list with this prospect on it. You've spent no money sending direct mail or other marketing collateral to this customer. You haven't spent any time or money nurturing the lead. It's even better if you find yourself in a position of having no competition. You're spared the temptation of discounting to win the sale. Your prospect's already gone through the Know-Like-Trust phase, so the total time of the sales cycle is reduced.

All of this adds up to a lower cost of sales. Less resources spent and a faster close mean a lower cost of sales. Referral business may very well be the most profitable business you ever close – even after paying a referral fee.

Of course, referrals have to be a win-win-win.

- **Your referral partner has to win.**

  You have to live up to the trust they've placed in you by providing an excellent experience to the customer. The last thing you want to do is create an unhappy customer. If you do – it's not just the customer who is unhappy; your referral partner will be unhappy, too, and your lucrative referral source will shrivel up and die right in front of you.

- **The customer has to win.**

  Your products, services, and pricing have to be a good fit for them. If you feel, at any point, that you can't provide what the customer needs, or you feel it's a bad match (for example, maybe your prices are outside their budget), or if there is anything that would be an impediment to the customer experience – let the customer and your referral partner know as soon as possible. Do so in a friendly and helpful manner so everyone leaves with a good feeling.

- **You have to win.**

  The referral has to be qualified and truly a customer who can afford and benefit from what you have to offer. The referral should represent a profitable opportunity for you unless there is a compelling business reason to discount in this case. It may be worth a discount to get into a new market or niche by serving this customer; or, it may be worth it to develop the referral partner because of future referral opportunities. But you may need to walk away if you see certain warning signs. For example, if the customer's budget and spending priorities mean they're always going to be stretched for dollars, or they're showing signs of becoming a nightmare customer – unreasonably demanding, disrespectful of you or your staff, or slow paying, it's best to nip the disaster in the bud.

Next up, you'll discover why, even though referral marketing is one of the eight wonders of the business world, you're probably not doing it.

What Seems to Be the Problem?

"Yeah, I know nobody knows. Where it comes and where it goes."
Aerosmith

For most business owners, referrals are the ultimate in serendipity.

"Fortuitous happenstance" or "pleasant surprise" it's all at once delightful and mysterious. You're thrilled to have the easiest sale of your life fall right into your lap, but really don't know how it happened. You don't even know when you'll get another referral, or where it will come from.

We call them bluebirds. Very exciting to see, but you have no idea where they came from, where they're going, and especially, how to get more of them to visit. When you think about it like that, you realize the least you could do is to throw some birdseed out on the grass, build a birdhouse or two, and do what you can to attract bluebirds to come back again and again.

How to do that probably sounds more than a little mysterious right now – or else you'd already be doing it. For sure, you don't have the magic wand to make bluebirds show up again – much less, making it happen at will.

Somehow This Got Left Out Of Your Plan

Business plan? Got it.

Marketing plan? Yeah.

Most business owners have these bases covered, but very few have an official plan in place to encourage referrals, nurture current referral partners, and find more of them.

It's a little shocking, this apparent aversion to taking the easy way to get more ideal, prequalified, warmed up and ready-to-roll clients. Don't you think?

Even though we all know referrals are the most profitable opportunities, we don't do much to encourage getting more of them. (Well, WE do, but you know what we mean.)

We don't do anything to get more. Not even a phone call now and then to people who've sent referrals in the past.

Certainly that bare bones tactic would be more fruitful than doing nothing!

But what if you upped the ante a bit, and actually created a program that rewarded people for sending referrals your way?

It wouldn't have to be complicated. You could just send a simple, sincere "thank you for the referral" message, and that would probably be WAY more acknowledgement and encouragement than your referral partner usually gets. But you could be a bit more creative and generous by sending an appropriate referral fee, or sending referrals to your referral partners when you can.

If you want more referrals, there's no better way to encourage your partners to send more to you than to reward them.

Of course, you'll never do that, if you don't see getting referrals as a replicable process worthy of your attention. Making referrals happen more often is going to require you to focus and take an active role.

If referrals are the bluebirds of marketing your business, it's time to get serious about how to attract more of them. With such a positive impact on your business, getting more referrals is worth the effort.

What impact could a constant stream of referrals coming into your business have? Imagine doubling or tripling the number of referrals you had last year, this year. Then doing the same next year. Can you see why the planning is so valuable?

If so, it's time to craft a referral plan.

Your referral plan needs to address three major specifics to work well:

- Who's likely to be able to send referrals to your business?
- How much money is a referral likely to be worth to you?
- How often should you communicate with referral partners?

By creating a plan, and then working it, you'll put yourself way ahead of the pack of your competitors who have probably never given a second thought to systematizing the referral process. Your plan will help you keep referrals on the top of your mind, which is the best place to make sure you take action.

The rest of this book will help guide you through the strategy and planning needed to create and implement a lucrative referral program.

So, if you're not convinced that referrals could have a profoundly positive impact on the health and vitality of your business, don't waste your time – just stop reading. Then, as long as you're not the jealous type, why not pass this book on to another business owner who'll see things differently, read it cover-to-cover, implement the plan, and have a year that makes yours pale in comparison.

But if the very thought of passing up some of the most lucrative and amazing business opportunities that'll ever come your way sounds ludicrous, and you're pretty much chomping at the bit to find out how to get more "at bats" and shorter sales cycles, more profitable engagements, and all the other great benefits that come from having referrals stream into your business, keep reading.

But Wait…

Before we go much further, you've probably got a little, nagging voice in the back of your head that's whispering reasons why this will never work. Might as well take that voice on right away and silence it with solid answers.

"What if I end up with a whole bunch of... well, horrible referrals?"

Ahh, yes. If you lack clarity about your ideal client and the type of referral you want to receive, you could easily end up with bad referrals. Think, strategize, and plan this part carefully.

Your referral partners would be working hard to send you a flood of new customers, who all happen to stink. They wouldn't be a good match for your products or services, and especially not for your pricing. You'd waste a lot of time wading through really bad leads.

That won't do.

Your referral partners have NO chance of sending you drool-worthy referrals unless they understand who your ideal customer is… and that certainly won't happen unless YOU can identify that dream customer.

Here are some points to ponder as you identify and then describe your ideal clients:

- What is their demographic?
- What size business?
- Where are they located?
- What industry are they in?
- What challenges are they facing… that you can solve?
- What sort of personality traits do they exhibit?
- How hands-on or hands-off do you like your clients to be?
- How much handholding do you like to do?
- How much do your services cost, and what level of income do your ideal clients need to have to pay for your services?

Think back to when you've had clients that were really bad matches for any one of these elements, and you'll see how important it is to get supremely clear on what your ideal referral client is like. Odds are, your last really bad client experience is not something you want to repeat – much less encourage.

If describing your ideal client seems impossible to do, you can back into that description by recalling bad client matches you've survived in the past. By describing what you don't want – ever again, thank you! – you'll see a reverse image of your ideal client. Simply do some reverse engineering from your description of your nightmare client, and you'll have a clear picture of your ideal client.

Being clear about your ideal client can help you prevent misguided referrals – those that are too big, too small, need something other than what you do, or who are too hard to work with – and help your referral relationship succeed and flourish.

Your referral partner needs to be crystal clear about who to refer to you. There's always the chance you'll still get referrals that are a poor fit: too big, too small, not quite on-target for what you do. While you're hoping to attract bluebirds, you may easily catch eagles or finches.

Catching the wrong bird could really throw you for a loop… except that you're so smart you've got a backup plan. You can count on the fact that some of the referrals coming your way will not be a good match. Plan ahead for them. Who else do you know who would be a great match for that prospect? Build a network of people you can refer out to so that, sort of like a syndicate of bird-sorters, no matter what bird comes your way, you've got someone who can take care of it.

Without a backup plan, you'll spend half your time explaining to badly matched referrals why you can't help them. That wastes everyone's time. It also makes you look bad, makes your referral partners look like they don't know what they're talking about, and makes the customer have to wait even longer to get a solution while they're off on a wild goose chase.

Nobody wants to waste time. If people are sending you referrals, they want the referrals to be successful, to help you and the customer, and to have a positive impact on everyone involved… not to turn into a pain in everyone's neck.

Who does your referral partner serve?

When you think about prospective referral partners, ask yourself:

- What kinds of customers does this potential partner serve?
- How many of these customers match your idea of an ideal customer?
- What are their characteristics?
- What percentage of your partner's customers fit your ideal customer profile?

Even if only about 10% of your partner's customers match your ideal client description, that's okay. You'll just need to educate your partner on why that kind of client is a good match, why the others are not, and how to know the difference.

Turnabout is the best policy, here. Make sure you understand your referral partners' ideal customer, too, so you have a clear idea of who to send their way.

Successful referral programs flow both ways. Make sure you send referrals to your partners, too… if they're a good match.

"But what if this gets lopsided?"
That can easily happen. Sometimes, referral relationships are one-sided. One partner's making referrals left and right, but the other one's not making any.

It can go either direction, and in some cases, it might be nothing to worry about. It might happen because they just haven't run across any customers who match your ideal client description – and better not to send anyone your way than to send the wrong customer. Right?

Or, it might be awfully quiet on their end because they're just not as committed to a referral relationship as you are.

If you think that might be the case, think about these questions:

- Did you set expectations correctly?
- Did you make it clear that you'd like to see referrals from them?
- Are they reciprocating in other ways – maybe by paying you a referral fee?
- Can you replace them?

If you're not getting referrals, and not getting a referral fee, and essentially you're not benefitting from the relationship, it might be time to make some changes. Why not develop a relationship with a new referral partner? Someone who serves the kinds of customers you'd like to have, and who's committed to building something that works for everyone.

"I know I do a great job for my clients, but how can I expect someone else to trust me?"
That's a good question! Trust can be risky.

Do these people know you? Have you interacted enough to build some trust between the two of you? If not, there's no way they'll entrust their customers to your care.

This is easy to fix, though. It's one thing to tell them all about how you've helped your customers, but it's much more powerful when that praise comes from someone else's mouth.

Here are some ways you can help your referral partners come to know, like, and trust you:

- Share case studies you've published and testimonials that have come in from your customers.
- Forward links to positive online reviews.
- Share good news about awards and certifications you and your team receive.
- Describe other referral relationships you have and examples of how they've created a win-win-win for everyone involved.
- Look to see whether you've got any customers in common from before when you started the referral relationship. Your happy customers are the most powerful proof in the pudding that you can offer.

"What if our business styles clash? Or, what if we just do business really differently?"

That can easily happen, and those differences can turn out to be disastrous if you're not careful. But it's an easy headache to avoid. Just make sure you spend time getting to understand your potential referral partner's business philosophy, personality, style, and processes before a referral ever changes hands.

Of course, those differences CAN turn out to be a positive experience – but that's pretty rare.

It's pretty simple.

You don't want nightmare customers. They drain your time and other resources and make you start to dread answering the phone, checking email, or even wishing you'd never seen or heard of them.

You especially don't want nightmare referral partners.

Three words of advice: Follow. Your. Gut.

If you see something that seems off, something that makes your spidey senses tingle, something that makes you make THAT face (you know, the one like when your dog just heard something weird), pay attention. If it looks bad now, it will only get worse once customers are involved.

"It might work, except I can never reach this person!"
"Staying in touch" might mean something completely different to your referral partner. Your definitions of "good communication" may be significantly different.

It doesn't matter whether it's business or personal, poor communication leads to trouble. In fact, the single biggest threat to successful referral relationships is poor or infrequent communication. It's important to interact frequently and productively with your referral partner to make that relationship strong and fruitful.

Lunch Leads to Leverage

A local business consultant invited three different key local business owners to lunch every month. The idea was to create her own wide network of local business professionals that she could connect if and when the opportunity ever arose.

With the invitation, she explained that it was important for her to have a network of locally respected individuals to draw upon and she always tried to invite individuals that had the potential to benefit from similar introductions. With this monthly lunch, the consultant typically expanded her close referral network by one or two people every quarter that added to growing her business and it also helped build her reputation in the community as someone who knew a lot of good people. She became a sought-after resource in the professional services space.

Kelly Weppler Hernandez
WH & Associates, Marketing Strategists

One chat's not enough.

You can't expect to have a single conversation that results in a highly profitable referral program. It takes ongoing communication to create an arrangement that works for everyone.

You need to educate each other about your products and services, about the problems you solve, and especially about how to identify your ideal customers.

You may need to take the lead and initiate regular conversations, but it's even better if you and your referral partners both commit to touching base regularly. At least once every month or two is ideal. Out of sight definitely means out of mind, so letting too much time go between contacts will dramatically decrease the momentum of your referral program, and put its success (and your relationship) at risk.

If you're working – either together or separately – for a customer you have in common, it might even make sense to touch base weekly or at certain milestones in your projects.

Even sending a quick email to keep your partner in the loop is a good idea. Something like this:

- "I wanted to let you know that your customer and I were able to touch base and set up a discovery call."
- "The discovery call is complete and your customer plans on making a decision before the end of the month."
- "Great news, the customer is signing on with me – I will keep you posted on how everything goes."

Your Definitions May Vary

You may need a translator. Different business niches speak their own language. Once the acronyms and jargon start flying, things can get confusing. ERP? CRM? Ha! That's nothing! Even the term 'referral marketing' can mean something totally different to another business owner.

You've got to make sure you're speaking the same language, especially when it comes to the particulars of what you and your referral partner do for your customers.

Here are a few examples:

- Both QuickBooks and SAP could be described as accounting software solutions. But they serve very different markets and are priced on opposite ends of the software spectrum. If you're selling SAP, receiving referrals for customers that are better suited for QuickBooks is a bad match.

- If you run a commercial construction company, receiving referrals for historic renovations is a mismatch.

- If your house painting company has highly skilled (and highly paid) painters who can meet the high expectations of residential re-paint work, a referral for new construction work where "entry level" labor is the norm may not be a good fit.

Make sure you're speaking the same language when you talk with your referral partner, that you know exactly what your referral partner means when using industry jargon, and that they understand what you mean, too.

You might even find it useful to create a reference sheet of terminology, along with a descriptive profile of your ideal customer. Having an easy-reference cheat sheet is a great way to ensure clarity.

Next up, you'll see how to build a referral marketing strategy for your own business. By the end of the next chapter, you'll be ready to take some action.

Renewable Referral Strategy

"Are we there YET?"

Anyone who's ever made and worked a plan

Entrepreneurs aren't exactly known for their patience. In fact, once we get a great idea, we usually turn around and ask, "Why isn't it done yet?" (and kind of mean it).

To build an effective referral program, you're going to need to do some planning first. And by planning, we mean actually writing your goals and plan down. Like, on paper.

Bear with us. You can dive into action later. Right now, the most important step you can take is mapping out your plan of action – a monthly checklist of action steps you can use to see how much progress you've made, and how much further you've got to go.

- **What do you want to see happen with your referral program?**

  One deal a month that comes as a result of a referral? One new referral partner added each quarter? Your goal should be realistic, and only you know what that looks like for your industry. For a restaurant, getting several new customers a day might be doable. For a professional service, maybe one a month is a reasonable goal. In the technology world, getting one a quarter or a year might be a more realistic pace. It all depends on the sales cycle that's typical in your field. Getting referrals definitely speeds up the sales cycle, but it doesn't erase it. Especially in complex sales processes, certain steps along the way still must be covered, no matter where the lead comes from. Your goals are up to you – just get them written down for now.

- **What do you have to do to meet those goals… each month? Each week?**

  Write your action steps into your plan. What will you do? When will you do it? Who will you contact? How will you identify and contact these people? What will you offer them? How often will you do this?

- **What results can you expect to see?**

  How much revenue will your company see if your plan succeeds? What percentage of your annual revenue will these referrals account for? Based on that figure, how much time and money will you allocate to working your referral plan?

Why Are You Doing This?

Your referral program will be a whole lot more profitable if you're crystal clear on your purpose for doing it. Having a clear purpose makes any plan more workable.

So, it's time to write a purpose statement for your referral program. (Stop groaning. It won't take long, won't hurt at all, and will help you get much better results.)

Here's an example you can follow as you create your own referral program's purpose statement:

"The purpose of my referral plan is to develop strong and long-lasting partnerships with other professionals that serve my ideal customers that will result in both parties having increased revenues year after year; and customers that are better served because of our referral relationship."

Don't drop your pen yet…

You also need a vision statement. Here's why: It will motivate you by reminding you why you're bothering with this whole referral plan in the first place. It's your chance to map out what's possible if you really work the plan you're about to create.

One way of looking at a vision statement is that it's a future state that can be measured. So, take the opportunity to go big here. It's okay if you feel like you're just guessing. What if you guess big and then make it actually happen?

We'll make it easy, and give you an example to follow:

"My vision for my referral program in five years is to have 12 referral partners that will participate in cooperative and collaborative joint marketing and generate 36 opportunities a year."

Measurable Objectives

Nothing more satisfying than getting it done, is there? If you're a list person, this is going to be especially fun because you're about to build a checklist that will help keep you accountable for working your plan.

Time to attach some numbers to your plan, and these numbers are going to flow from the vision statement you just created.

For example:

"In the next year, I'm going to _____."

Here are some ways you could complete that sentence:

- Identify 50 potential referral partners.
- Connect with my 50 potential referral partners on LinkedIn.
- Begin contacting 2 potential referral partners each month and add follow up calls to my calendar to keep the relationships moving.
- Create an ideal customer profile fact sheet I can provide to potential referral partners.
- Co-host 4 marketing lead generation webcasts with referral partners.
- Make 6 referrals to potential partners.

Remember, this will vary greatly from industry to industry. The more complex the sale, and the higher the price tag, and the longer the sales cycle, the longer this will take. The goal of referral marketing is to get more high-quality targeted leads, NOT to rush prospects through the sales funnel at an unnatural pace. Try to do that, and it's going to feel a lot like proposing marriage on a first date: too much, too soon. Set goals that match with the particulars of your business.

Keep these objectives where you'll see them. Sounds obvious, right? But we both know how easy it is to craft a great plan and then file it away for safekeeping… and never remember to look at it. Kind of hard to work a plan you don't look at daily.

Strategy Before Tactics (of course!)

Duct Tape Marketing Consultants' clients hear that phrase a dozen times if they hear it once, but only because it's so important. If you don't have a thorough understanding of your strategy, you are doomed to a costly and frustrating lifelong membership in the tactic of the month club. Without a strategy in place first, you'll chase every squirrel, be hypnotized by every shiny object, and do your best imitation of a hamster on a wheel – but you won't get the results you're after.

Here are the components of your master strategy:

1. What's in it for… everyone?

We talked before about how with a solid referral program everyone wins. The customer wins. You win. Your referral partner wins. The only way to make sure everyone wins is to make sure you first understand what a win looks like to each of the players. You already know what's in this referral program for you. Think about what's in it for the customer and for your partner. What benefits does each player get from participating in the program? Make sure you can articulate these benefits clearly and convincingly on demand.

2. Why would people refer you?

Why you, and not your competitor? This is all about your differentiator. What makes your product or services worthy of a referral? Why are you the best option out there for referrals sent your way? Why should your referral partners feel confident sending their customers to you?

3. Who do you want referred to you?

We're back to your ideal client. You need to be able to describe your ideal client clearly enough that your referral partners can spot them a mile away. You want your ideal client description to be so precise that your referral partners could quickly sort through a crowd of potential referrals and correctly sort them into "Yes" and "No" groups, so you only get referrals that are a good match for you.

4. Who's likely to send referrals to you?

Think about your referral partners. Are they more likely to be in B2B (Business to Business) or B2C (Business to Consumer) companies? What industry are they in? Why would they (in particular) send referrals to you? What do they do for their clients? How would your products or services complement theirs for these clients?

5. Who would you like to send referrals to?

No matter how carefully you craft your ideal client description, and how clearly you communicate it to your referral partners, you'll still find you get some inquiries from leads you can't help. They may be too small for you, too large for you, or may require a different skill set than what you've got. To make sure everyone wins, you've got to have a backup plan for referring leads that aren't a fit for you.

6. How many referral partners will you have?

You're not limited to working with just one referral partner – either on the giving end or the receiving end. Just as you've got an ideal client, your referral partners have ideal clients, too. Some of your clients will be better suited for one of your referral partners than another. Even if you'd like to send all of your referrals to your best referral partner, not all of them will be a fit. Maybe it's a bad match because of location. Maybe their backgrounds, skill sets, personalities, or beliefs will make them a poor match. Because of these variables, it's smart to have more than one referral partner in each business category you'll send referrals to.

7. Who's going to manage referral relationships?

This one's a question of accountability. You can certainly dream that your referral partners will follow-up with prospective customers, touch base with you regularly, and keep the referral stream flowing in both directions equally… automatically. But the reality is, you'll probably need to step up and lead the process yourself. Make yourself the best example your referral partners can see and follow. When you do this well, your referral partners will want to mimic the way you run your referral marketing system.

8. Give first, and you're more likely to get.

One of the best ways to start getting referrals is to start sending some first. The law of reciprocity says you should give first. Camping out on your referral partners' doorsteps waiting for them to hand referrals to you isn't in anyone's best interest. Instead, take the initiative to look for opportunities to send referrals to your referral partners. Generate opportunities to send to them, and you'll stay on their radar. Every time you send a referral their way, they'll want to return the favor. You'll become known as someone with a highly desirable network, and you'll find referral generation – in every direction – becomes easy and extremely rewarding.

9. Get straight on the benefits and beneficiaries.

You want to be sure everyone involved benefits from the referral. You might want to put pen to paper as you plan your match making. Think about each of the players: referral maker, customer, referral recipient. What benefit does each party get from the referral? Is a referral fee or reward the smart way to go? Is appreciation for the referral best shown with cash? Concert tickets? Cookies? How confident are you that the referral is a solid match that will be appreciated by everyone involved? The more thought you put into making sure this is a win for everyone, the more likely it is to work out well.

The Moment of Glory or… "Gulp"

About halfway through the first year of your new referral program, measure your progress.

If you've been working your plan, you've probably got some great results to report.

Your revenues are experiencing an uptick, you're getting more effective and efficient in how you seek out referral partners, you're getting better about looking for opportunities to send referrals their way. It's all coming together, and it's rewarding to see how far you've come. You look at how far you still need to go, and know you'll make it.

Or, maybe you forgot to look at your plan after creating it. You got distracted. You didn't stick to your plan, and ended up winging it… and it shows in your results. Gulp.

It's okay. Sometimes new strategies cough and stumble at first. Just pick up where you left off and go at it again.

No matter what results you see at the half-year mark, it's time to evaluate what you need to do next to meet your goals. It's also time to start thinking about your measurable objectives for year two of your referral program.

Managing Your Business

One of my clients, Jon, is a financial advisor working with large companies implementing 401k programs and other group benefits. Jon's business thrives on referrals but getting them on a consistent basis has been difficult for him. From our work together, he began to create an agenda for every business meeting, particularly new clients. He would outline 3-4 topics he wanted to discuss on the agenda and the last item would always be how we manage our practice. This discussion went through the different people on the team, the different tools they used to communicate and how they marketed themselves, which is through referrals.

Jon discovered that by having an agenda, he covered all of the topics necessary and he didn't skip the subject of referrals because it was on the agenda. He also found that the amount of referrals he received from new clients where he implemented this strategy increased because he was talking about how it related to managing his practice.

Debbie DeChambeau
Select Business Team, llc

Next up, you'll learn how to make 100% sure you're never THAT guy as you build your referral marketing program – you know, the one nobody wants to talk to for fear of being hit up for referrals. When you're done with this next chapter, you'll know enough to turn yourself into a highly-desirable referral partner.

The Ultimate Referral Experience

"She name names."

Chinese food deliveryman, Seinfeld "The Race"
(when Elaine got her boyfriend blacklisted from food delivery)

Your referral program can either make you a highly-desirable, sought-after business partner... or effectively banned from polite society.

After all, once you're working a referral program in earnest, you'll be on the lookout for people who can refer customers to you – and those you can send customers to as well. In a sense, you'll be adding 'matchmaker' to your unofficial job title.

Nobody Wants to Be THAT Guy

You've probably heard that you're supposed to be asking people for referrals – pretty much anytime you're in a conversation that lasts longer than .08 seconds. Some sales trainers even preach the three-foot rule, in which anyone within arm's reach is going to hear about your business – and if it's not a fit for them, you're supposed to ask for the names of three other people you could contact.

Follow this advice in your referral program, and you can pretty much plan on living out your days in solitude. And heaven help anyone who actually gives you names (although we all kind of have those few friends who understand if you throw them under the bus like that… and who will return the favor the next time they're pressed to give up names).

How to Become a Hub (and not get the snub)

While the idea of asking for referrals sounds so easy on paper, doing it in a way that's comfortable for everyone involved takes some couth – and some planning. The most fruitful referral programs also require excellent communication and an effective way of rewarding referral partners.

Do it right, and you'll become like the hub of a wheel, creating a comfortable rhythm of referral partners sending you business, and you sending business out to your network as well. Your referral program can easily become the single most lucrative marketing method if you do this right… and you'll get to keep your dignity and all of your friends.

A Value Add and Introduction All In One

When marketing a house painting contractor, I wanted to leverage a relationship with a paint supplier to make connections with interior designers. The supplier also wanted to build relationships with designers, so we jointly set up a "Designers Luncheon" and invited designers from a target list we developed. At the luncheon, the supplier gave a color trends presentation and the designers also saw a "getting to know us" presentation about the painting business. The contractor then had new designers to call on to give color consultations to homeowners.

When selling larger paint jobs, the contractor told homeowners that a consultation with a professional designer was part of the service they provided, thereby adding to the value provided to homeowners. This sales tool also benefitted the designers by introducing them to homeowners and thus creating new opportunities for the designers to sell other services. Lastly, the designers referred jobs to the painting contractor so the contractor had effectively extended "reach".

But that's not the end of the strategic referral progression. Next, the contractor worked with a couple of the designers as well as the paint supplier to jointly host a couple of "Breakfast with Designers" sessions in targeted neighborhoods. The goal was to create an event where area homeowners could come to get their painting and interior design questions answered by professionals, and to learn about all three parties hosting the event. This was a very low-pressure confidence- and trust-building tool that resulted in requests for quotes.

Jeff Stec
Tylerica Systems, LLC

Search for Referral Partners

We've already talked a bit about identifying your ideal client. We've touched on how you figure out who might make a good referral partner for you – they tend to serve your ideal client with a product or service that is somehow complementary or connected to what you offer.

You're looking for peas to go with carrots.

For example, a new business owner needs an attorney, an accountant, an insurance agent, a commercial printer, an office equipment dealer, a banker, a marketing consultant. You might look for referral partners in any of these associated products and services your ideal customer needs.

You may encounter referral partners in the course of doing business. You may already even have people who send customers your way, and they're a great place to look at implementing a more intentional program.

You might find these people in your usual networking circles, too, which is great because they already know, like, and trust you even if you haven't done business together.

Of course, you might also find some great referral partners on sites like LinkedIn by doing a search for people near you who offer products or services that would benefit your ideal customers. If you identify someone on LinkedIn who looks like a promising match and you don't know them, you can always check whether you've got any connections in common who'd be open to making an introduction for you. You could also ask for input from those mutual connections about the best way to pursue that person's attention or business.

Do what feels comfortable for you, and start today to build the habit of looking for two things: connections to prospective referral partners, and people you could refer to them.

Make Your Approach

The best way to approach prospective referral partners will depend on how well you know them, whether you've got a history of referring business to each other, and how marketing savvy they are.

You will probably need to do a bit of education on how the process works – or you could just pass this book along to prospective partners so they'll get a full understanding of how to make this work for both of you.

It's not a matter of asking everyone you come into contact with to give up three names of people you will pester until they buy or die. Instead, you're looking for professionals who share your idea of the ideal customer, someone you could work together with, someone with complementary products and services these customers want.

As you get to know prospective referral partners, ask about the types of problems they solve for their clients, what their ideal client is like, and how you might recognize someone this partner could help. When you find someone you'd like to try partnering with, you'll both be on the lookout for ideal clients you can send to each other. Your ears will start to perk up when your client asks questions your partner could answer, when customers ask for some product or service you don't provide – but you know someone who does.

Talk It All Out Before You Make the Introduction

You don't want to make bad matches. A bad match is a waste of everyone's time, hurting your credibility and your partner's in the process. It's going to be important to have a conversation before you send a customer to your partner.

Go back through your partner's description of their ideal client, first of all. But also discuss some of the less obvious points that will make for a great – or horrible – match.

- How much hand-holding does this client require?
- How formal are they in communication?
- Do they prefer daily updates? Are they very hands-on or do they want you to just do your thing?
- Are they fast in responding? Or do they often take a while to get back to you?
- What's the payment arrangement they're used to?
- Are the personalities a fit?
- Are they chatty or super-efficient (ok, abrupt!) in their conversation?
- Are there time zone differences that might be an issue?
- Do they prefer to meet in person, or to have virtual meetings?

If you were matchmaking to get two friends romantically involved, you'd consider whether they were compatible, whether they shared the same philosophies about education, money, children, and a lot of other variables before making the introduction. In the same way, try to foresee any twists in the road your partner might encounter in doing business with your customer.

For example, what if you referred a contractor to go in and do some trouble-shooting for a large organization. At the end of the job, the contractor would likely expect to be paid on the spot. The corporation, however, is likely to have a net 30 payment process. If an agreement isn't ironed out in advance – or at least a conversation to set and realign expectations – no matter how well the contractor performed his services, nobody's going to feel completely happy with the interaction. Possibly, all anyone will remember is that it ended awkwardly.

A conversation like this can help set realistic expectations and prepare your partner to succeed with this referred client.

Have Each Other's Backs

You can't anticipate every possible glitch. But by helping your partner have realistic expectations going in, you'll set everyone up to win.

You also want to establish an understanding of how to handle potential issues. Let's say your referral partner sends a customer your way. You start working together, and before long this customer starts complaining about your referral partner. Or, maybe you overhear something that would impact your referral partner's business. Now what?

Make sure you establish ahead of time how you'd both like to handle a situation like that. Maybe you make an agreement to keep each other in the loop, to ensure your referral partner has the opportunity to address any issues that you become aware of. No matter how you two decide to handle this unlikely situation, make that decision before it happens. By having that conversation ahead of time, you'll avoid a lot of stress from being in a potentially uncomfortable spot where you're left wondering what to do.

Having each other's back is not just about handling challenges.

Also be sure to pass along the compliments you hear. People are usually quick to complain, but less likely to compliment. Your referral partner may not hear the attaboys that your mutual client shares with you about your partner. It sure makes a difference to hear praise from a client – even if it's second-hand.

Thank You Very Much

The planning, asking, and prepping parts of the referral process keep your referral program running smoothly. This next part makes it more fun and virtually guarantees you'll see an ever-increasing number of referrals coming your way.

It's part good manners, part creative rewards – and by implementing this element of your referral program, you'll set yourself apart as an excellent referral partner. Word will get out, and you'll find more potential referral partners approaching you, eager to do business together.

First, and this should be obvious, thank your referral partners every time they send a client your way. A simple email message is fine for thanking them for the initial introduction. You can ramp up the effectiveness of your gratitude by putting it on paper, writing a little thank you note... stamp, envelope, ink... the works. It may be the only non-bill mail your referral partner gets. It speaks volumes of your gratitude when you take the time to write and mail a little note to thank them for bringing the opportunity to you.

A Little Something Something

If the referral progresses to the point where there's a sale, something more is in order. You need to be sensitive to any rules and professional ethics binding your referral partner, but one of the best ways to show appreciation for a referral is with a tangible reward.

Be careful not to create a problem for your referral partner by sending a reward that's more hassle than it's worth (or worse, one that lands them in hot water!). For example, in some fields, referral fees must be disclosed, or may even be illegal.

Even when it's not advisable to send a financial referral reward, with a little creativity, you can thank your partner in a meaningful and memorable way.

Don't be cheap. Referral marketing is far less expensive than most other ways you can get new customers – but it's not free. Count your referral rewards as part of the cost of sales.

Send a gift that is appropriate for the situation. For a promising introduction, maybe send a logoed item from your business. If the deal is sealed, send a much larger gift – it could be a goodie bag, some expensive candy, tickets to a ball game, or even a mail-order delivery of wine, steak, or lobster (although be sure this gift will be appreciated by your partner. Just imagine what could happen if you sent a live lobster-gram to an outspoken vegan.)

Make sure your referral rewards are enticing enough to spur referrals. You've seen companies that dangle a little bitty carrot as the reward for surrendering the names of a few friends. It's just not enough.

In most cases, your referral partners are primarily motivated by seeing you succeed, knowing you'll send referrals to them, and making sure their customers get what they need.

They're probably not even expecting a reward, but they will definitely enjoy and appreciate it.

In other cases, depending on the industry, the referral reward is absolutely expected. The more money involved in the transaction, the bigger the reward. This is more likely to be the case in a B2B environment. Make sure you have this conversation ahead of time to ensure you've both got a grip on the expectations of your arrangement. Your reward program may be cash-based and as simple as a certain dollar amount paid for a certain dollar amount closed – or it might be preferable to extend a specified discount for future purchases as a referral reward.

Be sure to reward the right party, too. Your reward should go to your referral partner, not the client. You've probably seen this in businesses that ask for referrals, then reward the new guy with a massive discount for being new. That's not a good plan, because it penalizes the long-term, loyal client rather than rewarding them for bringing in new business.

One other important point as you choose how you'll reward your referral partners: Always make the reward tangible or financial. Do NOT reward by giving your services. That's a sure way to devalue your services and attach a falsely low price tag to them.

You can get double the mileage out of giving a referral reward by doing it in public – or at least in the presence of clients or others who might be good referral partners for you. By publicly thanking your referral partner, you can subtly plant the seeds that will grow your referral program. You can do this at a public event, through social media, or even in your newsletter.

Look for ways you can meet your referral goals by rewarding the people who bring referrals to you. You might even be able to turn the process into a game, where the rewards are announced, so it becomes a bit of a competition among your referral partners. Adding a little competition can spark people's enthusiasm and motivation to participate.

Next up, you'll see how to nurture your ideal referral partners so they move from a place of "I don't know you… why should I trust you?" to, "Here's one of my very best clients. Please take care of them." It's not a journey of a single step, but it's one that you can start now and reap the benefits before you know it.

Referral Partner Prospecting and Nurturing

"Flaming enthusiasm, backed up by horse sense and persistence, is the quality that most frequently makes for success."

Dale Carnegie

There's only one reason you're still reading – because you're smart.

You get it. You're already salivating over the prospect of linking arms with an army of referral partners to deliver the best products and services known to mankind to a thirsty crowd… and to reap the profits of your joint efforts.

That's flaming enthusiasm.

Now for some horse sense and persistence, and you'll be on track for success.

Here's the thing: Some of your prospective referral partners are going to jump right on this the first time you mention it. Some, though, may take a little work.

Referral partners are just like leads.

Not all leads are ready to plunk down cold, hard cash on their first exposure to your products and services. Some need a little wooing, a little education, the steady drip, drip, drip of lead nurture. You don't expect your prospective customers to buy or die right on the spot; you're prepared to help them through the funnel so they arrive at the other side, knowing, liking, and trusting you.

Same deal with your referral partners-to-be. Even those who jump at the idea of partnering with you may not have a referral at the ready right then. Some may also need a little nurturing to catch the vision for a program like this, a little education to understand how to make it work, even a reminder now and then to take an active role in generating referrals.

You'll get the best results from your referral program when you create a system for nurturing your referral partners. They're just as busy as you are. They have a million and one tasks to take care of, too. You'll stay top of mind and get more referrals if you invest in a referral partner nurture strategy.

This is especially important if you're working B2B. Sometimes the B2B sales cycle is long, and the products and services are extremely niche-oriented, which can mean long gaps between windows of opportunity for referrals. By making sure you're still top of mind for your referral partners, you won't miss those opportunities to refer one another.

Here are some effective ways of nurturing those referral partner relationships so they stay healthy and fruitful:

Personal Outreach

It's tempting to go high tech with the whole referral program idea, because it's easier and takes less time. There are definitely areas in your business that are the perfect match for automation and tech. Referrals is not one of those areas. So if you're thinking about going that route, don't.

Really. Please don't.

Some things are best done the old fashioned way – with your fingerprints all over them. You'll get the best results by connecting personally with your prospective referral partners.

Positioning Yourself As A Resource

If picking up the phone and calling people is difficult for you, develop a strategy where people call you. This is easily done by positioning yourself as a resource to others.

For example: If you are selling payroll services, generally you are dealing with someone in HR or the CFO. What are the different challenges that these individuals encounter in the course of managing their departments? They might have employee benefit, investment, banking or time management concerns. As the payroll salesperson, do you know a fantastic banker, someone that shines in the employee benefit or investment world and a productivity coach? First, if you don't know these professionals, you need to go out and meet them and get to know them. Once you have put together a network of professionals you trust, position yourself as a resource to every client. If they have any business challenges, you have great people you can recommend. How nice would it be if the HR Director or CFO of a large company called you instead of you having to call them because they needed help with one of their business challenges? Would you be thrilled to receive their call? It means they are thinking about you and they believe you can help their business. Even if they haven't engaged your services yet, they are thinking about you and when they are ready for payroll, you'll be the one they call.

When you refer someone that can 'save the day' you become a hero and you won't be forgotten.

Debbie DeChambeau
Select Business Team, llc

Why? Because the success of your referral program depends on how well your referral partners get to know, like, and trust you. That's not impossible to do electronically, but is best done face to face if possible. If that's not possible, aim for the closest approximation you can.

Referrals are best cultivated in a high touch environment. It will take more than one contact, too. Don't set yourself up for disappointment by having the unrealistic expectations that you can walk into a networking event, meet some people, and sit back and wait for referrals.

Put yourself in their shoes – are you ready to transfer YOUR hard-earned trust with your contacts to someone you just met?

Your first conversation is an excellent first step – but it's not the only step. You still have to cultivate the know-like-trust aspect of your relationship. That takes time.

Referral marketing is not nuking coffee in a microwave. You'll get the best results by following a process of gentle, persistent, collegial nudging and nurturing. Stay in touch, build the relationship, and do what you can to stay top of mind for your potential referral partners.

Pick Up the Phone

So, there's this thing called a phone. Sure, it lets you play games with angry or flappy birds. You can check the weather, or delight your 1,007 friends with pictures of your adorable cat. You can practically run a business from the palm of your hand. But it also has this strange old school function: You pick it up, punch in a few numbers, and talk to someone. Freaky, but very effective.

If you're not a hermit, you're scratching your head right now. In case the world of introversion is foreign to you, here's a brief: Some people would prefer to automate, outsource, and connect in bulk whenever possible rather than have to deal with people. That actually works ok in many aspects of business – but not for referral marketing.

However, every minute you spend talking with a prospective referral partner will be fruitful, if that helps motivate you. You might even find it enjoyable if you create a routine for talking with these partners on a regular basis. Second best to meeting face-to-face, the phone will go a long way toward helping your partners know, like, and trust you because of having the opportunity to hear your voice.

Mail and Email, Too

Snail mail and email play an important role in nurturing your referral partners – but don't think for a moment that you can use them as a way to avoid spending time building the relationship. These are ways you can supplement your efforts to connect, not a substitute for face-to-face or phone conversations. Be sure to personalize your messages, making them obviously one-off creations rather than a mass mailing you might send out to your marketing list.

Getting a personal (rather than junk mail) piece of mail via the postal service may be a bit of a novelty these days. It'll leave a positive impression and contribute toward your effort of staying top of mind.

Whaddya Say?

Whether you do it in person, on the phone, or by snail- or electronic mail, you've got some goals to shoot for in your communications. You want to get to know each other better, and especially get to know what makes each other's business tick. What are you each great at? What are your ideal clients like? How would you recognize excellent referrals to send to one another? What do you think about working together as referral partners? Do you share the same vision for what you could create together?

You may find it helpful to run through each other's sales funnels as if you were prospects. Share the marketing you do to reach your prospects, because by going through it first-hand, you'll each get an education on what you both do, what your best prospects are like.

Motivating Reward that Leads to an Upsell

I had a client who was a residential cleaning company and after doing their client surveys, it was apparent that while everyone said they "would" refer, most of them were not giving referrals. When asked, "Why?" they did not really have a reason. Experience taught me that it just wasn't easy for them to refer and it may have felt awkward. My client did ask for referrals when she was getting feedback after cleanings, but it just was not happening.

So we decided it was time for a formal referral program. For a single referral, the client would get their refrigerator cleaned out top to bottom. Everything would come out of the fridge and every little corner with gunk would be scrubbed. For their next referral, the client would get an overhaul of their pantry. Same deal, everything comes out of the pantry, the shelves get wiped down and it all goes back in an organized fashion. For a third referral, the client would receive a complementary pressure washing of their driveway and walkway coordinated with a strategic partner. The idea was that the referring client would get an added service on their next visit and each time it would be something different and valuable. Valuable in terms of saving time for the client and giving an extra touch. The best part is that these services were part of an upgraded package so it was a great way to introduce the client to additional services.

Rosie Taylor
Rosiemedia

Bear in mind that every communication you send needs to build trust. Just starting to prospect your referral partners? Already have some sending you referrals? Celebrating a referral partnership that's lasted for many years? No matter what, make sure your communications pass the "trust test" and help your partners trust you more.

Don't rely on a slick sales pitch – instead, build credibility so your partners feel increasingly more comfortable entrusting their referrals to your care.

What You Need to Know, and Why

As we discussed already, setting realistic expectations is critical for making this referral program work. There's more to it, though, and as you get to know your referral partners better, there's more to discuss to ensure the whole referral process goes smoothly.

Some other topics you'll want to touch on as your relationship progresses… most of these are double-duty topics, meaning you'll discuss how you'll work together and how you work with your customers.

- **Sales Cycles:** How long does it usually take for a prospect to move through the funnel and reach a buying decision? How does this timeline compare in your businesses?

- **Billing:** What would your clients prefer (other than not being billed at all, of course)? If you and your referral partner have products and services that are connected, would it work best for the client to pay you each separately, or to pay once and the two of you work out making sure you're both paid? Is there an expectation of being paid on the spot? Or is net 30 the norm? The context and norm will determine what's appropriate, and it's best to know in advance.

- **Contingencies:** What possible glitches might pop up during your client's experience with you, and how can you run interference for both the client and your referral partner to make sure the client's experience is the top priority?

- **Fine Print:** Talk about any terms and conditions connected to referral fees paid, if that's relevant for your particular arrangement. For example, is there a time period that has to pass – such as a refund period – before you'll pay out? What if the product is subscription based? How does that impact your referral fee?

- **Deliverables:** Be sure to cover the details of what each of your customers actually get when they buy from you. You don't want to give a client the wrong idea about what your referral partner will and won't do – or for your new customer to be confused about what they're getting, either.

- **Details:** Talk about the nitty gritty, even down to how and how often you'll meet. This goes for your referral partners and for any customers you refer to one another. For all of us, time is the most valuable and least flexible resource we've got – make sure anyone you do business with understands how yours is allocated.

- **Marketing activities:** How will you promote your customer (if applicable)? How will you promote your partner (definitely applicable)?

- **Measurable objectives:** How will your customer know you've been effective on their behalf? How will you measure the success of your referral program together?

- **Challenges along the way:** What will you say if you encounter a potentially divisive situation? How will you have each other's back to make sure everyone gets what they need from this partnership, including the customer? It may even be helpful to script how you'd handle certain foreseeable challenges so that you'll know exactly what to say and do, and that your referral partner has already agreed to the plan.

Rock Solid Always Beats Rocky

By communicating openly and regularly, you'll build a strong relationship with your referral partners. By building your whole referral program on rock solid relationships with these partners, you'll get really good at referring ideal customers to one another.

You'll also preempt a lot of awkwardness that can happen in the course of doing business with humans, which is sometimes a surprisingly rocky road. Cementing your professional bond with your referral partners will go a long way toward making sure you both work for the benefit of everyone involved. This bond will help you think clearly if things ever veer off-course with a customer.

Without that solid relationship, and a lot of discussion of the particulars – in advance – it can be more than just awkward when challenges arise. A complaining, non-paying, defecting, or otherwise difficult client, if one appears, now becomes just a passing instance, rather than a threat to what could be a beautiful friendship.

Next up, you'll find out how to ramp up your referral results by joining forces with your referral partners. There are ways you can both get exponentially more referrals just by working on this together.

Beyond Revenue Sharing

"Louie, I think this is the start of a beautiful friendship."
Rick Blaine, Casablanca

Beyond "You Scratch My Back…"

If you choose your referral partners wisely, you'll find that referrals flow naturally from simply paying attention to what else your customers need in addition to what you provide. You may find yourself sending referrals to your partners on a regular basis to provide, together, everything that your client needs – kind of like planning, building, and decorating a house together with other tradespeople. It might even look like an assembly line of sorts, as your customer gets an assortment of needs met all because of connecting with you first. You steer them to solutions you'd rely on yourself.

The more your business grows, the more your referral partners' businesses grow.

Theoretically.

You can make that more of a certainty if you cooperate on joint marketing, too. You'll still do marketing activities on your own, but if you catch a vision for how joint marketing can benefit you both, this can be an instance where the whole is greater than the sum of its parts.

People like less hassle.

The promise of getting everything in one place is why we're willing to subject ourselves to shopping at Target or the mall. (A dubious bargain once you weigh in the hassle of the crowds, the parking lot, and the feeling of being herded like cattle – but stick with us here, because the point still holds.)

Very few products and services are islands. Every peanut butter has its jelly, and it's the same with your business – there are other products and services your customer needs that go hand-in-hand with what you're selling. When your customer has an excellent experience with you, they want more. They wish you could handle the add-on products and services they need. With your referral program, you come as close to one-stop shopping as anyone can hope for – the ultimate win-win-win.

What If You Could Turbo-Boost the Process?

By doing some cooperative marketing, you can generate more business together than you might do on your own. Plus, it'll be this extra-excellent kind of business – the kind that features more of your ideal clients getting more of what they want, while you and your referral partners get the satisfaction of delivering results and generating some of the most rewarding revenues ever.

You're probably going after a lot of the same ideal clients, anyway, so why not join forces with your referral partners to turn up the heat on your marketing? Think about how you could use the following to market together:

- Live events
- Educational seminars
- Webinars
- Online networking

Two Heads Are Better than One

Just by planning and executing a joint marketing plan, you'll both get better at generating new business – together, for sure, but you may also learn some new marketing tricks, too.

It's going to be especially important to hold each other accountable here, because, as we see in nearly every business, marketing often gets short shrift in small- and mid-sized businesses. Just by knowing your referral partner is going to ask whether you've done what you agreed to do, marketing-wise, you're more likely to actually do it.

Plan Your Plan

Rather than winging your joint marketing activities, you'll get better results – and make accountability a snap – by creating and using a marketing calendar together. A simple way to do this is to create a shared document – a Google Docs spreadsheet is one way to go – that will be easy to access, update, and view for both of you.

For each marketing initiative, record your goals (it's okay if they feel like guesses, because they are), the action steps involved, the due dates for these action steps, and who's doing what.

If you think about it, having someone else "out there" marketing on your behalf is a pretty sweet deal.

In fact, most referral partners would jump at the opportunity to plan and do cooperative marketing activities, but in many cases, they're just not sure what kinds of activities might work. That's why it's good to work on this together. Each of you has probably had marketing tactics that worked really well – and you may spark ideas in your partners that end up being more effective than anything you've done in the past.

Gather a Team of Relevant Resources

Two of my clients have approached referral marketing in a creative way. One is an accountant, and the other is a tech company.

The accountant created a partner page on the firm's website. The list of partners includes other professionals a client might need: an attorney, a health insurance agent, a business insurance company, and a retirement planner. As any of these partners meets with a new client, this list is furnished to the client in case they also need their services. The group of partners often does group presentations together, speaking in front of highly-targeted audiences. Because of their combined expertise, it's pretty much guaranteed attendees will come away with valuable information as well as resources they can call on when needed.

The tech company has created an ambassador program in which a team of specialized consultants mediates a technology forum where customers can ask questions. Through this forum, they get leads and opportunities to share, provide added value to the customers, and build a community where they are positioned as experts.

Ray L. Perry
MarketBlazer, Inc.

So, what works?

The list of marketing activities that are a good fit for your partnership will vary based on the type of business you are in and where your ideal clients hang out. You may come up with some really creative marketing ideas you can do together. The basic idea is to serve as a host to your customers, introducing them to your referral partners as a trusted resource. You're sort of like a host or hostess at a party, making introductions and connecting people.

Some Starter Ideas

Press Releases: You can both get mileage out of press releases announcing that you are working together. You may want to frame the announcement in terms of choosing your referral partner as a preferred vendor. Focus on the benefit to your customers in providing access to vetted resources and a more comprehensive solution.

Advertising: You could go in on ad space together, sharing the space and the expenses. Together you may be able to swing the cost of a much larger and more prominent ad than you would have taken separately.

Direct Mail: This works especially well for postcard marketing. One side for you, and the other side for your partner. This way, no matter which side is face-up when your prospect receives the piece, you've both got a good shot at new business.

Email Marketing: You can easily share your referral partner as a trusted resource in your emails. This is an excellent opportunity to offer an exclusive deal on your referral partner's products and services to the subscribers on your list. Just be sure not to sell or rent your list out, which is a sure way to irritate people and prompt them to unsubscribe.

Trade Shows: Whether you share booth space or have spots near each other, you can always steer prospects to one another. Also consider going in together on a spectacular giveaway and share the leads you generate by having attendees complete a contact card.

Conferences: A tag-teaming game plan with your referral partner will give you twice the opportunity to connect with the people you need to meet. As you talk with other attendees, you can provide your partner with third-party credibility, making introductions for anyone who seems to fit the ideal customer persona.

Newsletters: You could dedicate a segment of your newsletter to feature a column by your referral partner. This not only gives your readers the opportunity to get to know your referral partner – it's also an excellent way to provide high-quality content that you didn't have to create, while making your newsletter more valuable to your readers, to boot.

Webcasts: What if you arranged with your referral partner to produce a webcast where attendees got some valuable, exclusive information that they need? By hosting this virtual event, you give value to your customers, your referral partner is edified while presenting, and your customers get solid information from an expert they'll quickly come to know, like, and trust.

Customer Events: One of the best ways to keep your customers as long as you want them is to reward them and provide extra benefits to thank them for their loyalty. This is easy to do by scheduling special events for customers throughout the year. Make these events even more valuable by having your referral partners contribute in some meaningful way that exposes your clients to them, while giving value in their first contact.

Prospect Events: Jointly host a live event where you provide information, a preview of services, or something else where prospects can get a taste of what you and your referral partners offer, and you and your partners will find new customers. You might even consider holding an event together that benefits a local charity – a good way to make for a win-win-win... win!

Blogging: Guest blogging with your referral partners is an efficient way to expose your readers to the full range of products and services they can access because of their connection with you. This tactic has two added benefits: adding unique, valuable content to your website (that you didn't have to create!) and borrowing from each other's credibility to firmly cement your business and your partners' businesses as experts.

Social Media: Be sure to introduce your social media followers to your referral partners on a regular basis. In addition, social media is a good way to build connections, and it's easy to share your partners by cross-sharing the content they create. Put the spotlight on your partners by highlighting what makes them great. It's often easier to toot someone else's horn than your own, and when you give an honest and glowing review or comment about another business' products and services, it speaks volumes to anyone listening.

Reputation Marketing: If appropriate, be sure to create glowing online reviews of your referral partners' businesses. Also, when your customers report back to you with their good results from working with your referral partners, be sure to coach them on how to share their experience and leave an effective online review to help spread the word.

Pool your resources and put your heads together to mastermind and launch joint marketing projects. You'll find you can reach more ideal clients more easily and serve them even better than if you were on your own.

Up next, you'll see how to build the single most important element in a referral partner relationship. Without this, your referral program will struggle to get traction.

Your Renewable Referral Program

> *"These go to eleven."*
> **Nigel Tufnel, Spinal Tap**

The Care and Nurture of Your Referral Marketing Machine

The stuff of legends, the promise of a stream of highly-targeted and prequalified prospects is enough to get most business owners as excited as a dog that just heard the familiar sound of the UPS truck's transmission a few blocks away. It's go time! You bark, you chase, you run with all your might.

But what happens when you catch the truck?

Your referral program will only thrive if you know what to do with what you catch. This involves taking care of your referral partners at every turn — from nurturing them through the discovery and launch of the partnership on through reinforcing their confidence in you by taking excellent care of your new customers. Creating a delightful experience for your customers and your referral partners has a cyclical effect – their happiness over how you do what you do leads to more opportunities for you to do it.

Thank You, and THANK YOU!

A good referral program acknowledges the referral at two points: When the referral is received and when the referral closes. A company I worked for would send out a "thank you goodie box" when the referral was received. The box included a logo'd mug filled with candy and a hand-written thank you note. If/when the referral converted to closed business, the referral fee was sent along with another hand-written thank you note.

The idea was to reward at the moment the referral was given, so that even if the referral did not result in closed business, the act of making the referral was rewarded in a small way. The logo'd mug was an important element – a branded way to stay top of mind. The referral fee, given when business was closed, was generous enough to make an impression and a reasonable amount of money to pay based on revenue gained from the referral.

Dawn Westerberg
Dawn Westerberg Consulting, LLC

Your Referral Machine Runs on Trust

Trust is fuel here. Fear is the brake pedal. The more your referral partners feel they can trust you, the more likely they are to send business your way. It's an intangible with a lot of power over how your referral program plays out. You may never know what fears your prospective partner has, but you still need to put them to rest if you want this to work.

They may never verbalize these fears, but that doesn't mean they aren't present.

Here are some common fear-based obstacles that can derail your partners and program:

- What if you screw up, and I lose a client because of you?
- What if I refer to you and the project becomes a train wreck?
- What if it turns out that you're full of it, and you over-promise and under-deliver?
- What if you offend my client?
- What if you over-charge my client and they get mad at me?
- What if, even if you've done a good job with certain types of customers, you get in over your head with

this new one I send you? (especially risky with B2B clients)

All of these fears have a central theme: They send you a referral. You screw up. The customer is unhappy. They look bad.

Knowledge Burns Fear

You can bolster your referral partners' trust in you by educating them directly on your products, services, methodology, and style. But you should also show them the view from behind the curtain when you can by sharing case studies, including them on client visits or conferences, and anywhere else that they can see you in action with your clients.

Any referral partners who've had the opportunity to work with you in the past as your client will have an even better idea of what it's like working with you, and will trust you because they've got first-hand knowledge of how you operate. For some referral partners, it's going to take a lot of time and testing to be sure you're a good match for them and their referrals. For others, the vetting process won't be quite so arduous.

It takes time and history to build trust, so you'll need to be patient and consistent as your prospective referral partners arrive at the conclusion that they can trust you not to let them down.

Clarity Boosts Credibility

Communication ills will stop your referral program in its tracks faster than any other challenge you might imagine. There are so many opportunities for things to go well, or to go horribly wrong, where communication is concerned. There's what you meant to say, what you actually said, what they thought they were hearing, and what each of you remembered about the conversation – that's a lot of opportunity for misunderstanding.

Good communication doesn't just happen by itself. You'll want to bolster trust through building clear communication practices. Aim to set and manage expectations so everyone goes in on the same page, discuss eventualities so you know what to do when the unexpected happens, and talk about the rules of engagement for your partnership. These conversations are too important to skip. Communicate regularly and succinctly with your partners to set the protocol for the partnership.

Meet Referrals Where They Need You

One of my clients is a water, fire, smoke, and storm restoration company. It has developed a referral marketing program in which they partner with those businesses that could also be needed when their customers face an immediate need for help.

Let's say a tree falls on your roof. You need a tree removal company, but you probably also need a roofer. You may also need a water damage restoration team, an electrical contractor, a plumber, and a construction team. We have built a referral network where these complementary services help clients by recommending one another, which results in better outcomes for the homeowner as well as increased business for each of these related service businesses.

The restoration company is also a registered preferred provider with insurance agents and adjustors, so now truly get most of their business through referrals.

Ray L. Perry
MarketBlazer, Inc.

Documentation Eases Duplication

Any process worth doing in or on your business is worth documenting. By creating templates, process documents, checklists, and information packages you can access and rely on to keep your business processes running smoothly, you eliminate the need to reinvent the wheel every time you face certain situations and opportunities.

Stuff that gets written down gets remembered. Processes and policies on paper are more likely to get followed. Agreements that get inked get fulfilled. When the info you need is at your fingertips, distributing it is a snap.

You're busy in your business. Details tend to get slippery – especially once you start working with multiple referral partners. Trying to use your brain to hold onto important details is a sure way to let them slide through your fingers and crash to the ground. Writing it all down is a surefire way of eliminating uncertainty, minimizing misunderstandings, and building a consistent track record of delighting your referral partners and the customers they send your way.

Now's the time to start getting it all on paper.

You'll want to create the following documents and info packages so they're within arm's reach when you need them. Some of these documents will be most useful in-house and others for giving to your referral partners:

- Description of your ideal client
- Description of your ideal referral partner
- Your marketing kit, which includes:

- ○ A description of your ideal client
- ○ What problems your ideal client is facing, that you solve
- ○ What results your clients can expect by working with you
- What your new client intake process looks like
  - ○ Do you make the first contact by phone? In person?
  - ○ Do you prefer to have your referral partner set up the introduction? Make the introduction with a 3-way call? In person?
  - ○ Is there a questionnaire or other intake form you'll use to facilitate getting the information needed to move forward?
- Description of your referral program and how it works
- Client information packages, including:
  - ○ Marketing materials
  - ○ Packages and plans
  - ○ Sample client agreement

Forms Capture Details

You may also find it helpful to create some templates and forms to use with your referral partners. Since the details of your arrangement with different referral partners may vary, you might want to use a form that allows you to enter the specifics on a case-by-case basis.

Be sure to cover:

- How you'll work together with your referral partner, if applicable.
- How will invoicing be handled? Cover who sends the invoice, how it will be paid, when it will be paid – all of the money details.
- What are the deliverables and expectations of the engagement?
- How will you and your partner communicate throughout the time you have this customer in common?
- What expectations does each partner have for one another?

Your processes will evolve as you get more experience working together and with other referral partners. The more you're able to document and standardize the processes, the easier it will be to manage and multiply your referrals.

Up next, it's time to thrust this whole referral marketing concept out into the cold, hard world. You've got a few choices to make, and this last little bit of input will help you make them wisely.

What Happens Next

You're at the end of the book. That means you've invested valuable time reading these ideas – time you could have spent doing just about anything else on your never-ending list of must-do tasks.

This is the moment of truth.

You get to choose what happens next, and it seems like there are three possibilities:

1.   **You can do nothing.**
     You close the book, put it on a shelf, and go about your business. We really hope you don't do that. Your time and attention are too valuable to waste by reading and not taking action on what you've read.

2.   **You can go out and start building your own referral marketing program now that you know what to do.**

This is a great idea, and in fact, nobody can build a referral relationship for you. That's a task you are uniquely qualified to carry out. If you'd like help designing your specific referral strategy beyond what you've just read, or even if you'd just like some accountability as you do it, any one of the authors of this book can help you.

3.   **You can divide and conquer.**

If you're already wearing too many hats in your business, it's time to take a look at what you alone can do best, and what you can hand off to someone else (so you can do what you do best!). If you'd like to take marketing execution tasks off of your plate, freeing yourself to go build those referral relationships, that would be an excellent opportunity to engage one of the authors. You work your referral relationships; we handle the rest.

Since we believe so strongly in the value of implementation, we'd love to hear about the steps you take in building your own referral marketing program.

Why not share your progress with us by posting a comment on our group Facebook page?

https://www.facebook.com/RenewableReferrals

Whichever course of action you take (other than doing nothing!), we're rooting for your success. If you'd like any of the authors to present at an upcoming event – or to introduce the whole referral marketing program concept to your potential referral partners, let's talk about making that happen.

Be sure to subscribe to us on YouTube where you'll find a series of quick and helpful videos:

www.youtube.com/renewablereferrals

About the Authors

Founded in 2013, the Marketing Results Crew was launched with one mission at its core: To provide customers with strategy before tactics while continuously building the kind of awareness that sparks lead generation among ideal prospects. Crew members bring a variety of experiences ranging from local B2C to international B2B marketing, and are committed to ongoing education and implementation of best practices in business. Many of the group members have spoken at national conferences, local workshops, and webcasts, and have written and been published in prominent marketing books and publications.

Deborah L. DeChambeau
Select Business Team, llc
www.selectbizteam.com

Known as 'The Queen of Networking,' Debbie DeChambeau has x-ray vision for turning ordinary connections into business referral opportunities. Using her networking savvy and marketing insight, she has a unique ability to communicate ideas that facilitate business growth. A business architect, national speaker and founder of Select Business Team, llc (selectbizteam.com), Debbie delivers high-impact customized referral strategies for turbo-charging sales professionals and business owners to greater profits. She has helped hundreds of business professionals create referral opportunities.

Before starting her own business, Debbie worked for international networking organizations like Business Network International and eWomenNetwork, teaching professionals how to deliver their message and build a network of ongoing referrals.

For more information about Debbie, visit:
www.renewablereferrals.com/debbie-dechambeau/

To see Debbie's special offer for Renewable Referrals
readers, visit: www.renewablereferrals.com/select-biz-team

Ray L. Perry
MarketBlazer, Inc.
www.marketblazer.com

Ray L. Perry heads up MarketBlazer, a technology based marketing agency specializing in lead generation and lead management. Ray's experiences as a high-tech marketing executive and online marketing consultant merge to serve his clients in an environment that is creative, challenging, respectful and innovative.

Ray is the author of *Guide to Marketing Your Business Online* (2011). He combines proven marketing processes and a strong technology background with the latest in Internet, social media and mobile marketing tactics to develop solid long-term marketing strategies for his clients. His goal with marketing is simple and straightforward: to help every client's business thrive.

As a Certified Duct Tape Marketing Consultant, Ray helps his clients develop marketing strategies to find prospects that have a need for their products and services, and engage those prospects to know, like, and trust his clients, becoming long-term customers. This can further result in these new customers referring Ray's clients' to other potential customers with the same need or problem.

For more information about Ray, visit:
www.renewablereferrals.com/ray-perry/

To see Ray's special offer for Renewable Referrals readers, visit: www.renewablereferrals.com/marketblazer

Jeff Stec
Tylerica Systems, LLC
www.TylericaSystems.com

Jeff Stec is a former high-tech engineer and executive who has also "worn all the hats" owning and operating several small businesses. Additionally, Jeff has held Adjunct Instructor appointments at the college level. In his spare time, Jeff enjoys figuring out ways to apply new technologies to solve business problems.

As a Duct Tape Marketing Authorized Consultant, Jeff melds the consulting and project management skills gained during his high-tech career, his educational orientation, and the real-world experience gained from operating his own businesses. Jeff has cultivated a strategic partner network that allows him to meet the full range of marketing needs from strategy development through tactical implementation. He can operate as a coach, advisor, or Virtual Marketing Department for his clients.

Originally from Vermont, Jeff has lived in Austin, Texas since 1993. Jeff and his wife Carol operate Tylerica Systems, LLC which is named after their children, Tyler and Erica.

For more information about Jeff, visit:
www.renewablereferrals.com/jeff-stec/

To see Jeff's special offer for Renewable Referrals readers, visit: www.renewablereferrals.com/tylerica-systems

Rosie Taylor
Rosiemedia
www.rosiemedia.com

Rosie Taylor's entrepreneurial spirit dawned in her teens with her newspaper route. Even when she was employed at a full-time job, she still built websites for small businesses at night. She had the good fortune to be exposed to marketing from giant corporations like Nikon down to her own wedding coordinator business. As a full-time marketing consultant, Rosie often helps her clients develop their own referral programs while leveraging the power of online marketing.

Rosie's experience has resulted in a skill set of creative ideas mixed with business acumen so that her clients can launch authentic programs that continually grow their business. She regularly volunteers her expertise to teach SCORE participants how to build their own marketing strategy and is sought after to speak about marketing in front of many small business groups and trade associations throughout South Florida.

For more information about Rosie, visit:
www.renewablereferrals.com/rosie-taylor

To see Rosie's special offer for Renewable Referrals readers, visit: www.renewablereferrals.com/rosiemedia

Kelly Weppler Hernandez
WH & Associates, Marketing Strategists
www.whandassociates.com

Kelly Weppler Hernandez is a marketing strategist who focuses on lead generation for small B2B technology companies. Kelly has instructed small businesses in the skill of marketing alongside Duct Tape Marketing founder John Jantsch, been interviewed by the American Marketing Association, and written articles for several small business magazines. After building the strategy, she works with clients to build and execute a marketing action plan that combines high tech and high touch to deliver success.

She says the technology is necessary to get it done and track your efforts, but the personal touch is vital in building a business people will remember.

Kelly is a Master Duct Tape Marketing Consultant and the founder of WH & Associates, a marketing consulting firm in Orange County, California.

For more information about Kelly, visit:
www.renewablereferrals.com/kelly-weppler-hernandez/

To see Kelly's special offer for Renewable Referrals readers,
visit: www.renewablereferrals.com/wh-associates

Dawn Westerberg
Dawn Westerberg Consulting LLC
www.dawnwesterberg.com

Dawn Westerberg is the president of Dawn Westerberg Consulting LLC, a marketing strategy consultancy. She works with business owners and nonprofit professionals to develop marketing strategy, identify ideal prospects, and then use both inbound and outbound marketing to generate leads and develop a strong online presence. Her career includes senior management positions including Vice President of Marketing and Sales at Sage, Open Systems and Lawson. Dawn is based in Austin, Texas and serves organizations in the United States and Canada.

Dawn is a Certified Duct Tape Marketing Consultant. She speaks frequently around the country on the topics of Social Media, Marketing in the New Normal, Emergency Lead Generation, and Creating an Online Presence. Dawn publishes a blog on B2B Marketing at dawnwesterberg.com.

Dawn was named one of Twitter's Top 75 Women by Bit Rebels.

For more information about Dawn, visit:
www.renewablereferrals.com/dawn-westerberg/

To see Dawn's special offer for Renewable Referrals readers, visit:
www.renewablereferrals.com/dawn-westerberg-consulting

Request Your Referral Marketing Audit Today

To thank you for reading Renewable Referrals and to help you implement what you've just read, we'd like to offer you a complimentary Referral Marketing Audit. This tool will help you get a realistic idea of how you're doing at using referral marketing to grow your business.

All you need to do is visit:
> www.renewablereferrals.com/referral-audit/

Complete the form you'll find on that page.

Once we receive your completed form, you'll hear back from one of us within one business day and you'll receive a written evaluation of your personal Referral Marketing Audit. In that evaluation, we'll make some specific suggestions as to how you can put the power of referrals to work for you in your business.

We're looking forward to help you grow your business through referrals!

Made in the USA
San Bernardino, CA
22 September 2014